P9-DBR-947

WAY
DOWN
YONDER
ON
TROUBLESOME
CREEK

WAY DOWN YONDER ON TROUBLESOME CREEK

Appalachian Riddles & Rusties

by
James Still

pictures by Janet McCaffery

G.P. Putnam's Sons New York

To
Teresa Lynn
Michael
Chad
and
Jerry Dean

Bring your gifts and graces and tell your secrets to this lonely country child.

—Sarah Orne Jewett

There was a time not so long ago when Troublesome Creek country was a land of creekbed roads and winding mountain trails, and travel was by sled, wagon, horseback, and shank's mare.*

The 67-mile stream flows across the counties of Knott, Perry, and Breathitt into the headwaters of the Kentucky River, fed from coves and hollows and valleys bearing such names as Tadpole, Push Back, Possum Trot, Dismal, and Gritty, and by hamlets called Dwarf, Fisty and Rowdy. The folk spoke in a manner handed down from their forebears in England, Scotland, Ireland, and the Black Forest of Germany. Many of their words, nowadays strange on the tongue, are found in *The Canterbury Tales* of Geoffrey Chaucer and the dramas of William Shakespeare.

*To travel on foot.

To make their bread, the people grew corn, grinding it at water mills. They raised sheep for wool and spun and wove many of their garments. They sat in chairs of their own handicraft, slept in rope-strung beds on goose-feather ticks. Though the ridges were veined with 'coal, most chose to burn wood.

They made soap of ash lye and grease, dried and sulfured apples, holed-up potatoes and cabbages in the ground for the harsh months. Their medicines were brewed from wild herbs.

Schools were in session following the laying-by of crops in July, closing in February in time for the grubbing of sprouts before the spring planting. The fields were often so high on steep hills, the jest had it that they were planted by shotgun. It was possible to fall out of a patch and break a bone. Proud was the day a boy was accounted man enough to handle a plow, a girl expert enough with a needle to join in a quilting.

Boys made marbles of pebbles in potholes of flowing streams. Girls fashioned dolls of corn shucks. For both there were johnny-walkers to stride about on, wild grape vines for swinging, bow-and-spikes to shoot. The fragrant

plum-granny* was cherished, the flowers of the bubbybush† tied up in handkerchiefs to "smell

on." Tadwhackers** delighted themselves with zizz wheels,‡ spool tops, and ridey horses.§

In autumn hickory nuts, walnuts, and chestnuts were gathered. During the first full moon in June, when the signs of the zodiac were favorable, there were sapping parties. A black birch was felled, the inner bark scraped off and mixed with sugar for chewing.

And then the braver ones dared a wild ride on a sheath of bark the length of the skinned tree. Bean stringings, corn shuckings, and

---

*A fragrant, inedible vine fruit. ‡A twirling button operated by strings.
†Sweet shrub (Calycanthus). §Seesaw.
**Small children.

house raisings were social events for the elders.
And on many occasions there was homemade
music. Fiddles were sawed, banjoes picked, or
dulcimers* strummed—often to accompany old
ballads or for square dancing.

Before log fires on winter evenings young
and old roasted "Irishmen,"† chestnuts, and
Adam-and-Eves,** told tales about the
legendary Jack and his exploits, stories of
witches and ghosts, and feats of daring by their
pioneer kin who had come into Kentucky along
the Wilderness Trail blazed by Daniel Boone.
They sprung riddles and pulled rusties.

The riddles had been handed down from
their ancestors, many of them so obscure that
the answers were lost. There were many
versions, and as apt as not to change from one
mouth to the next. The rusties were turns of
wit, tricks of words, or common pranks.

Thus did these Appalachian folk live and
work and pleasure themselves on Troublesome
Creek and its tributaries within living memory.

*A folk musical instrument.
†White potatoes.
**Tuber of the Puttyroot orchid *(Aplectrum hyemale).*

Riddles
&
Rusties

The last earthly things I expect to see:
    A mouse picking a cat's teeth,
    A jailhouse plundered by a thief,
    A mule plowing of its own accord,
    Old Horned Scratch praising the Lord.

Twelve pears hanging high,
A dozen Hatfields riding by;
Now Each took a pear
Yet left eleven hanging there.

One of the Hatfields
was named Each

Way down yonder at the forks of Troublesome
    I found a pile of timber;
I couldn't stack it, I couldn't whack it,
    For it was awful limber.

Sawdust

"Spell 'geography.' "

"Hit's a word a mile long and
I hain't learnt that far
in the Blue Back Speller."

"Why, spell it Sporty Creek fashion."

"How's that, old son?"

"George Enoch's old grunting
razorback* ate persimmons here yesterday."

Riddle, riddle, randy crow,
I can't move but here I go;
Two black hands to cover my face,
Key to set my daily pace;
Though I'm one you'll likely shelve
I can point you twice to twelve.

Clock

*A breed of pigs with sharp backbones.

Old John Snipp has two heads and a dandy pair of legs, and as a cut-up he has never met his match. He's as strong as iron; still you can handle him with two fingers.

Scissors

I went to the woods and I got it,
I brought it home in my hand because I
  couldn't find it,
The more I looked for it
  the more I felt it,
And when I found it
    I
      threw
        it
          away.

Thorn

Spell
"butter"
in **4** letters.

Goat

Beefhide, Zilpo, Mouthcard, Stop,
Sideway, Redash, Spoutspring, Drop,
Select, Tobacco, Eighty-Eight, Dimple,
Sixty-six, Soldier, Threelinks, Sample;
Gad, Gabe, Widsom, Zag, Weed, Speck,
Stepstone, Bigbone, Snap, Bent, Keck,
Bromo, Blackjoe, Sip, Honeybee—
How many are in Ken-tuck-ee?

Every one;
All are towns

Two lookers,
Two hookers,
Four down-hangers
And a fly swatter.

Cow

Three brothers were crossing Troublesome
on a day in June. One had No eyes, one No hands,
and one wore No garments. The brother with No
eyes saw a gold guinea on the bottom. The one with
No hands picked it up. The one with No garments
put it in his pocket.

The brothers were
of a family named No.

What travels the roads standing on its
head and never takes a drink of water?

Horseshoe nail

If a cowbird lays five eggs at best,
How many eggs in a cowbird's nest?

None; Cowbirds lay their
eggs in the nests
of other birds

Nobody under the shining courts of
  heaven has seen it,
It can whistle but can't talk;
It can make you cry and dry your eye.

Wind

I met a tailor packing* a goose,†
A hen with twelve diddles** running loose,
Trailed by a turkey wearing a noose.
How many fowls had he for his use?

Fourteen

*Carrying.
†Tailor's smoothing iron.
**Young chickens

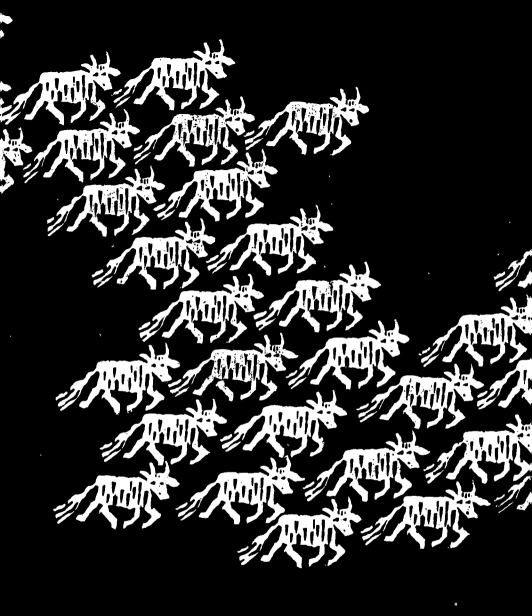

Crooked as a blacksnake, level as a plate,
Forty thousand oxen couldn't pull it straight.

Creek

Ten little stuck-outs,
 One got a blow,
Knocked its roof off
 (Another will grow),
Hear the wee master cry,
 "Oh! oh! oh!"

Stubbed toe

My pappy gave it to me, though it belonged to my grandpaw. Despite my having it, my grandpaw kept it. And proud as I am to have it other people use it more than I do.

My name

Way down yonder in Honey Gap
I met a gent as red as a cap,
A twig in his hand, a rock in his belly,
Unriddle this one and I'll shake like jelly.

Cherry

Listen, Big Buddy. What is black as a crow, stands on four legs, smokes a pipe, and has to be fed morning, noon and night?

Cookstove

Whim-wham, shim-sham, jog-along, shift,
There's a weightless thing you can't lift.

Hole

Ready to walk, long tongue, no talk.

Shoe

At three months of age it has a full
set of teeth and golden hair. At six months
it is snaggle-toothed and bald-headed.

Ear of corn

One 'possum baby,* a bearded goat,
Seven sawbucks,† a hundred-pound shoat;
Of how many critters may I gloat?

Two

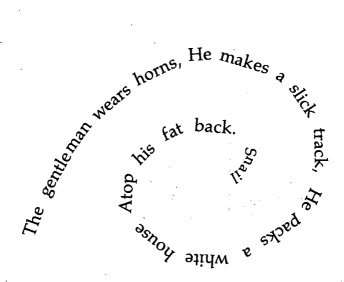

The gentleman wears horns, He makes a slick
track, He packs a white house Atop his fat back. Snail!

*A term of affection for an infant.
†Dollar bill

A host of eyes buried deep,
Eyes staring yet cannot peep,
Eyes that never close in sleep;
And oh! the cruel, cruel hand
Gouging the eyes into a pan.

Potato eyebuds

There was a man of Adam's race
Who had a certain dwelling place;
Wasn't in heaven, wasn't in space,
Wasn't on earth the Good Books tell,
Who was this man and where did he dwell?

Jonah in the belly
of the whale.

Awful clever,
Feeds any and everybody,
Quiet when there's not enough,
Groans when there's too much,
And never eats a bite.

Table

Which side of a fox hound has
the most hair?

The outside

Why should a body mind his tongue in a cornfield?

Awful lot of
ears listening

Its blooms are bells that will not ring,
A bush wherein a bird daren't sing,
Fruit that even pigs won't swill,
Yet folk never get their fill.

Pawpaw*

*Pawpaw—a wild fruit with bananalike flavor. It is a
folk belief that birds won't sing in a pawpaw bush
and pigs won't eat the fruit. There are many folk
beliefs on Troublesome Creek. For example: "Gray
mules never die," and "If it thunders in January, it
will snow that same day in May."

Opens like a pocketbook,
Closes with a click,
A tent of black spread in air
On a walking stick.

Umbrella

A witty* was passing through Colson Gap packing a heavy poke† of salt. Said he to himself, "Upon my word and deed and honor! I'll snap my backbone ere I get to the house." He set his poke down to rest and directly he struck a thought. He took the poke and began to put in something. He put in a whole big lot of somethings. Then off he tramped and his load got lighter by the minute.

What in tarnation did he put in the poke?

Holes

*A simpleton.
†Bag.

A house

Without a mouse;

No cat, no rat,

No griddle, no fiddle,

No plunder, no thunder;

A house without sleepers,

Crickets or neepers,
  Yet!

A house with a roof,
And I have proof;
A house that will travel—
And for you to unravel.

Turtle

Pick a short word with five letters,
add two more letters and make it shorter.

Short-er

William is the poor chap's name,
He calls at dusk, and all in vain;
He would be flogged (to hear him speak),
But you couldn't tip him in a week.

Whippoorwill

Its red eye blinks, the pale tears flow,
And what its sorrow none may know.

Candle

He didn't ask for it,
    Yet he got it,
He didn't want it,
    Still he had to take it,
But now that he's got it
    He wouldn't part with it
For the ball of the world.

Bald head

 BOW WOW WOW WOW

The worldly wonders I'm dying to see:
  The moon barking at a dog,
  A root rooting up a hog,
  A berry pie buzzing a fly,
  A mossy rock sighing a sigh.
And what had I rather do than dine?
  Spy a pretty girl
  And she be mine.

    Why does Troublesome Creek get restless
  once in a while and flood its banks?

It has rocks in
its bed

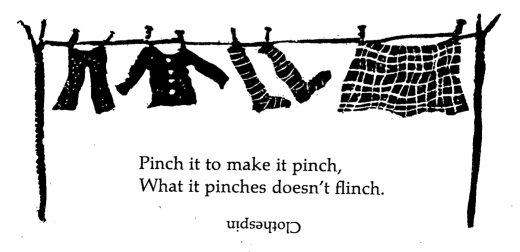

    Pinch it to make it pinch,
    What it pinches doesn't flinch.

Clothespin

As I rode across the Hazard bridge
I met a man in the rain,
He touched his hat and drew his cane,
And in this riddle I tell his name.

Andrew

The clock struck XIII
On Halloween.
What time was it?

Time to take the
clock to the tinker

Two legs have I
    And what will confound:
Only at rest
    Do they touch the ground.

Wheelbarrow

She has droves of friends and a smattering
of enemies. Rivers of tears have been shed
on her behalf, yet she never broke a heart.

Onion

At two I thought it was a tree,
At twenty it reached above my knee,
At seventy-five
    I
      bend
        over
          to
            it.

Walking stick

Fireflies can't figure,
Mites can't write,
Or gnats indite,*
Still I know right well
A bug that can spell.

Spelling bee

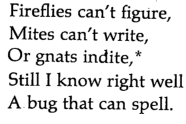

*To compose—as a verse.

What grows in winter
   with
   its
   head
   hanging
   straight
   down
And dies in summer?

Icicle

Five jaspers a-hunting,
Five foxes a-running;
Two foxes got away—
Just how I cannot say—
And the race stood then:
Three foxes, five men.
What time was it?

Five after three

"Spell cat backward."
"T-a-c."
"Now, no, fiddle-head."
"How, then, brother fox?"
"C-a-t- b-a-c-k-w-a-r-d."

Can't find it in ocean, or in ground,
Or in air, or in town,
Yet it's here and everywhere.

Letter "h."

Pot belly,
One dark eye,
Poke its ribs,
Make it sigh.

Stove

Rising up,
Pitching down,
Touching neither sky nor ground;
Lifting high,
Slanting low,
Having neither head nor toe.

Seesaw

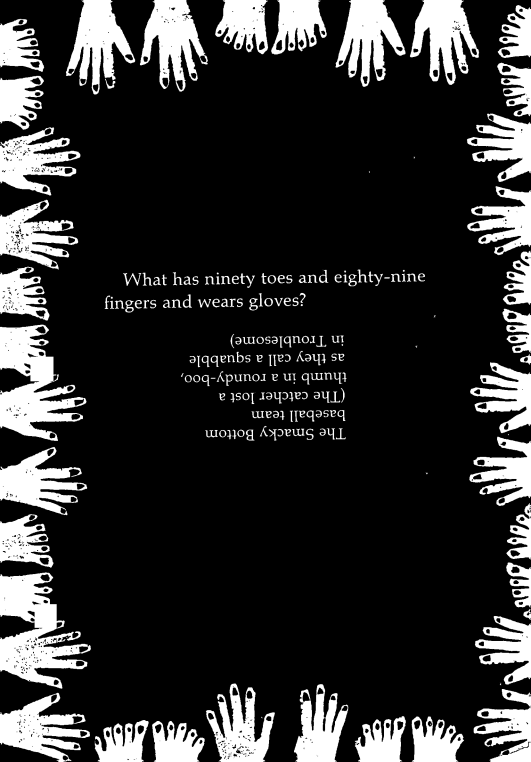

What has ninety toes and eighty-nine fingers and wears gloves?

The Smacky Bottom baseball team (The catcher lost a thumb in a roundy-boo, as they call a squabble in Troublesome)

They're put on the table, cut and served,
and never eaten.

Declared Jerb Logan, the squire of Turkey
Hen Hollow, "I aim to take down my rifle-gun and
hang on me all the powder and shot I can bear up
under, and clap on my squirrel cap, and hie me to
Possum Ridge. I'll be cooned if I don't!"
And Jerb, who was deaf in one ear and couldn't hear
out of the other'n, said, "You crave to know what
varmints I aim to hunt? Air ye deef? I've told
you already and I'm a gentleman who chews his terbacker
just once."
What game was Jerb after?

John Bud Whitley planted his
beans in the black of the moon and they came
up the same day. How could that have happened?

Chickens got into the garden

It's needed to fix breeches,
Rib-bonnets, shirts and such-as;
It can make blood fly,
Prepare shroud* should you die,
And ho! ho!
It can put you in stitches.

Needle

There is a toe that will never suffer a
corn or be pinched by a tight shoe.

Mistletoe

*Burial garment.

When first I wear my dress in spring
It is a yellow fey,
In fall my garment's whitest down,
In winter blown away.

Dandelion

Red-headed,
Box-bedded;
Well to know
It flies mad
The least blow.

Match

I have teeth and yet can't eat,
Can't crunch corn or bread of wheat,
Still I'll fix you fairly neat.

Comb

I rode water, I repelled rain,
When I died I felt no pain,
And once I was stony dead
I stuffed a pillow for your head.

Goose feather

Why does a chicken cross the road?
Reason's the same for cow or toad,
For lizards green or May bugs pied,
Just to get on the other side.

Big at the bottom,
Little at the top,
Thing in the middle
Goes ker-flippety-flop.

Churn

From room to room the lady dances,
Across the house she lightly prances,
The hem of her gown brushes the floor,
Upstairs, downstairs, through every door;
Her partner swings her with airy zest,
Then leans her against the wall to rest.

Broom

Use three letters to
  sour cream
  grow whiskers,
  ripen pears,
  turn tadpoles into frogs,
  boys into men,
  mules into fools.

A-g-e

I spent two round dollars for a
second-hand pair of firedogs.* I bought
a poker and it lightened my pocket seventy-
five cents. A turn of kindling cost me
every whit of a dime. My only need then to
keep me warm through the winter was three
cords of wood. What do you figure they
came to?

Ashes

*Andirons—metal support for wood in a fireplace.

Long and thin,
Nubbed at the end,
Has a twin.

Shoestring

Bloom of stink-jim,* a mangy skunk's hide,
Blue-flies and lye and miner's carbide,
Coddled with corn and left to rot,
Stewed and brewed—and what have you got?

Troublesome Creek moonshine

Red though I be
I'm green to thee,
Black my name
In maturity.

Blackberry, which is red
before it becomes ripe.

*A tall, poisonous weed with rank-smelling foliage and
trumpet-shaped flowers.

There is a suit you cannot wear,
Not made of wool or cotton or hair,
A suit that brings peculiar pain,
And yet to win it is to gain.

Lawsuit

Sixteen letters in "Troublesome Creek,"
Spell it or I'll give your nose a tweak.

I-t

What state bordering Kentucky has a hoop
on each end and a hello in the middle?

Yonder it goes, here it comes,
Uphill, downhill rain or sun,
Served many a hoof and leg
Yet has never moved a peg.

Path

Eyes moon-yellow,
Head that will twist,
Guess your fool head off
You can't name this.

Owl

"What's your name?"
"Pudding N. Tane
Ask me again and I'll
Tell you the same;
Ask me no questions
And I'll tell you no lies,
Keep your mouth shut
And you'll catch no flies."

Of weavers the best am I,
My own yarn do I supply,
None can match me, did they try,
To wear my cloth is to die.

Spider

Houseful, yardful,
Can't get a spoonful.

Smoke

Black as midnight, heavy and thick,
Long flat tail straight as a stick.

Frying pan

Spell water with three letters,
Heat it and spell it with five.

Ice, steam

It'll bite you. But if you know its
name, you'll understand what to do the next
occasion you meet.

Flea (flee)

Old Dial Thomas built a barn of poplar
logs. And would he use iron nails? Now, no.
Not by your bowlegged grandpaw he wouldn't.
He said they would draw lightning and set it
afire. So maul* in hand, he went driving wooden
pegs all over the place. But hey-o! Where did
he hit the first peg?

On the head

*A hammer with a wooden head.

Round as a pumpkin,
Shaped like a cup,
All Troublesome Creek
Couldn't fill it up.

Flour sifter

Way down yonder in the creek-side patch
Sits a yellow homeseat lacking a thatch,
Within the house another of white,
And a gold house in the white wedged tight;
Forty yellow houses within the gold,
Forty-three houses by my count all told.

Pumpkin

There's red calf in the meadow,
and she'll eat hay on any day, but
give her a drink of water and she'll perish.

Fire

I found a thing good to eat,
White and smooth and ever so neat,
Neither flesh, nor fish, nor bone,
In three weeks it ran alone.

Egg, which a hen
hatches into a chick
in twenty-one days

Black when they dig it,
Red when it's used,
Gray when it's thrown away.

Coal

In summer I'm dressed fit to marry the
Queen of Sheba.
   In winter I'm naked as a wheat straw.

Tree

Round as an apple,
   Flat as a plane,
      (Hole in my pocket,
         Beggar again.)

Coin

I went to the miller's,
   His wife was dyeing,
      His little one crying,
         His daughter rockaby-ing.
How many were there
At the miller's a-dying?

None

Riar Tackett was the Dirk postmaster until his eyes failed tee-totally. Claimed he wore his sight out figuring quare place names on envelopes. I reckon he learned the name of every city, crossroad, and hooty hollow earthly. And so did his wife and his son Goodloe, who helped with the mail. Now they were pretty anticky, the three of them. Not so stiff-necked they wouldn't cut a rusty. And sometimes they played a game they called "Kentucky Post Office." Like one evening when son Goodloe said:

I've got it in my head to put on my *Vest* and *High Hat* tomorrow, *Load* a *Barlow* in one pocket and *Watch* in the other, and put on my *Tearcoat* and *Drift* along to *Walhalla* as *Happy* as a *Butterfly*. Come *Sunrise, Bigreddy!* I'll be *Nigh Ready.*"

"That's *Fairplay*," Riar said. "You'll have good *Prospects* if it doesn't *Rain*. My advice is use a little *Enterprize* and go *Barefoot* and live *Cheap*. Take my *Gunn* and *Airdale*, *Dinguş*, and hie you to *Dog Creek* and *Catch* yourself a *Red Fox*, *Badger*, *Raccoon* and an *Otter*. And you can *Break Ice* and *Fixer Fishtrap* for *Sunfish*. And you can *Wing* a *Kettle* of birds for *Relief* : a *Dove*, *Raven*, *Pigeon*, *Quail*, *Sparrow*, and a *Redbird*. Use *Energy* and it'll work a *Drop* of a *Miracle*."

"*Ono*," said Goodloe. "You're a *Kidder*, else you're *Cranks* after *Game*. Think I'm a *Zap*! I don't *Mize* and I do nothing *Halfway*. It takes *Cash* to *Win Praise*. You can't *Grab Awe* and *Pomp* without a *Penny*. I'd as soon *Limp* to *Stamping Ground* and sit on a *Stump*. I aim to go to *Pleasureville* and take *Alice* and *Mousie* and *Polly* and *Susie* and *Alberta* and *Picnic* at *Lizzielane*. They've said, '*Ucum*' and '*Welcome*.' *Gee* what a *Bunch*!"

Riar's wife pitched in. Says, "Going *Ordinary* to *Fancy Farm* will put a *Jinks* on you. The *Poindexter* are *Quality Peoples*. They're *Tip Top Grade*. First take you a *Bath* and make yourself *Fragrant*. Watch out for a *Viper* at *Hot spot*, and behave *Lovely*."

"My opinion," said Riar, "you'll go *Rightangle* to my *Proverb*. You'll act *Fisty* and in the *Longrun* wind up in the *UZ Callaboose*. You'll *Lay* there till *Christmas*. That'll be the *Climax*."

"*Nonesuch*," said Goodloe. "I'll *Bet* a *Beefhide* to a *Turkey*, or a *Gimlet* to a *Gander* I won't drink a *Julip* or even pop a *Cork*. And you know I don't *wax* to *Tobacco*. I'm not *Wildie*.

Riar's wife said, "*Stop*. Show *Charity* and *Skip* the *Disputana*. Grin and stay *Lax* and *Humble* and *Nonchalanta*. *Be Goody* and hold no *Illwill*."

"*Bybee*," said Goodloe, "I won't be gone *Long*."

"*Good Luck*," said Riar. "You're the *Monkey Eyebrow*!"

(All the italicized words above were actual post offices in the Kentucky postal guide for 1923. Today many of the post offices have been discontinued, but the *places*—towns or hamlets—remain.)

The Author

In the early 1930's James Still moved into an ancient log house in Knott County, Kentucky, accessible only by eight miles of dirt road and two miles of creek bed. He came there from his native Alabama by way of the University of Illinois and Vanderbilt University, where he earned degrees. Working there quietly, supporting himself sometimes by farming or teaching at Morehead State University or serving as librarian of the Hindman Settlement School, Still has written stories and poetry that have received great critical acclaim. He writes about things he knows well: the people, the land, the ways of life of rural Kentucky. Some of his best verse has been collected under the title *Hounds on the Mountain*, some of his best stories in the book *On Troublesome Creek*, and many readers are discovering today in its paperback edition his beautiful novel first published several years ago, *River of Earth*.

The Artist

Although Janet McCaffery lives in New York City, where she pursues a distinguished career as an artist, she flees to the country as often as possible. Born in Philadelphia, she received her Bachelor of Fine Arts degree from the Philadelphia College of Art. She has illustrated many books, her most recent from Putnam's being the popular *Cristobal and the Witch* by Jan Wahl. *The Swamp Witch*, which she both wrote and illustrated, was chosen by the American Institute of Graphic Arts as one of the best-designed children's books of the year.